# Music Runs Through It

Written by

## Lonnie J. Good

ElderBerry Publishing
CMP Publishing Group, LLC

Lonnie J. Good

ElderBerry Publishing is a division of CMP Publishing Group, LLC. The
focus of this division is community and family history, but is not limited to that genre. Full color children's books are also published under
the ElderBerry imprint.

All inquiries, including distributor information, should be addressed to:
    33 Appleway Road
    Okanogan, WA 98840
email: lonnie_good@yahoo.com
        or
ElderBerry Publishing
    27657 Highway 97
    Okanogan, WA 98840
email: info@cmppg.org
website: www.cmppg.com

ISBN13: 978-1-937162-08-5

Library of Congress Control Number: 2014951743

# Dedication

To my bride: You worked while I wrote. Sit back now and read, and I'll go mow the grass. To my children: Here are some things I wanted you to know. To my mom and dad: If it were not for you, I would have experienced nothing. I love all of you.

William Samuel and Eva Adela Good

# Table of Contents

In the Beginning 7
New Sounds 12
1604 Township Street 15
Marblemount 20
The Cascade River 21
Hippie 26
Walking 28
Wind River 30
The East Side 33
Life On The Ranch 34
Pitch Black Darkness 40
Short Stay At Bible Way 43
Between a Boy and a Man 45
Stripes of The Fool 47
Mountaintop Meeting 48
Night Vision 51
Fast Cars 53
Wings For Christ 58
Facing Fear 61
Getting Back On 68
Too Soon To Fly 70
Time Alone 72
Solid Ground 74
Our Little House By The River 76

# Foreword

"Music Runs Through It" is more than just a "good read." It is more than just an autobiography! More importantly it is the emotional, spiritual adventure of a boy becoming an authentic man. Toxic manhood is based on living "outside in." Genuine manhood is living "inside out."

Lonnie Good has discovered a most inspiring truth; whatever failures, disasters or losses that have occurred in our experiences can be transformed into spiritual building stones to become the incredibly strong spiritual and psychological foundations of life. His heartbreaks become stepping stones to discovering heaven on earth.

His greatest battles were not with the outside world but with the deep inner struggles of heart, mind and soul. The problem was not the problem; the problem was how to interpret the problem.

Lonnie Good interpreted life through the template of God's word, God's wisdom and God's purpose. He discovered that music (hope) runs through the rivers of darkness and light. The bottom line of that hope is Jesus Christ, the hope of the world.

Yes, Lonnie was at times broken, but out of brokenness he, with God's help and great mentors, became a wounded healer who now celebrates life in Goodstock Music Festivals, Wings for Christ and in a daily celebration walk with God. How Awesome!

Thank you, Lonnie, because your journey is our journey and your stories will resonate with many wonderful people who will now discover God's wonder in all of life.

II Corinthians 12:9, "But God said to Lonnie, 'My grace is sufficient for you, for my power is made perfect in weakness.'" Lonnie has discovered with Paul, in my weakness I am made stronger.

Rev. Ronald J. Deegan
First Baptist Church of
Mount Vernon, Burlington and the Cascade Christian Center
located in Washington State.

My younger sister Cheryl, our Mom, my older sister Tricia and me.

# In The Beginning

Painting a picture of life without a father could be like reaching for a palette that is void of color, with no way to create contrast or variation. The lines are blurred and the shadows are only dark. My heart yearned for his company for many years.

Fortunately for me, my heavenly father filled my palette with all variations of color. I had more brushes than I could use. I created harsh and stark realities. Other times the brush strokes were soft and gentle, creating very faint, nearly invisible images. The surface, on which I painted, sometimes indescribable scenes, is called my life.

Dad's death resulted from a plane crash in which he was acting as a spotter, on a search and rescue mission with Civil Air Patrol. I will cover this in more depth later.

Come journey with me, if you will, over the last 56 years of painting pictures, ever changing landscape, danger, fear, anger, love, and discovery. Maybe we can find a laugh or two, maybe even a tear, a leaky eye in the middle of a sticky world that needs some lubricating.

My name was given to me by both my dad and mom. Mom is still here with us, celebrating her 82nd birthday this very day, December 21, 2013.

She named me Lonnie, after one of her nephews whom she loved. My middle name, Jay, was chosen by Dad; it was the name of a preacher that he liked. This brings to mind one story that has always caused me to grin. Mom shared with me an experience that she had with Dad while attending a church service.

Apparently it had been a while since the pastor had seen Dad in church, or if ever he had. Whatever the case he leaned over and said, "Why Sam, what are you doing here?" Dad's response was to stand up, look over at mom and say, "Let's go, Eva." Pretty much sums up how not to greet someone if you want them to feel welcomed.

My first memories of music are vivid. Our family would join with others from the Baker clan to share time and sit down and eat together. It was typically a yearly reunion that was hosted by my Aunt T and Uncle Roy Brookshire, at their home in Lyman, which was eight miles east of Sedro-

Woolley. Someone would have to pick us up and then return us home from the reunion as Mom never owned or drove a car.

Uncle Roy and Aunt T

Their home was once uprooted from its place where the oil refineries now reside near Anacortes. Uncle Roy bought it at auction for pennies on the dollar, placed it on a barge, then had a tug or paddle wheeler tow it across Puget Sound and up the Skagit River.

My uncle, though uneducated, was a man of means. He simply worked his way up and out of poverty to a place of stability and good standing in the community. Their home always seemed so rich and plush; they were the royalty of our family, or at least through the eyes of this child.

Being poor was not bad in itself, but the resulting gap it creates between you and the people who have money and things that you don't, can create awkward moments. It's typically not the poor who look down on the wealthy.

"Awkward" is being made to feel as though one is "less than" simply due to circumstances that are out of one's own control, and being made to feel as though you do not matter, kind of like a subspecies of human.

Fortunately, there are great joys in being poor, like being able to find treasures in places you would have never looked. Or hearing harmonies for the first time and having the realization that you were given the ability to create those same notes, tones, and harmonics.

It's hearing the marriage of the sounds of an acoustic guitar and a mandolin and an accordion all supporting the voices of people who otherwise seemed silent.

It's finding the indescribable beauty in nature that surrounds us at all times. It's following a meandering river up around the next corner or climbing up over that next set of rapids to the sights and sounds that await you.

It's searching for and finding the truth that is mixed with all sorts of "other" ideas about any and every thought and aspect of this life. It's learning through the trials how to be content with little.

Music had a way of taking my very quiet and reserved aunts and uncles and turning them into the very fun loving and incredibly optimistic and passionate people that they were.

Let's face it, there were thirteen children supported by one coal miner. Shoes were not mandatory in the summertime. My people knew what living close to the earth meant; there were no silver spoons at our tables. Lessons were learned the old fashioned way and one had to know how to use his own boot straps to aid in recovery from one of life's many bogs.

Music had a way of bringing magic into the room. It had a way of bringing something out of anyone who would only participate with it.

Mom is the youngest of those thirteen children, all of which have passed at this point in time. So the times of seeing my family together were short-lived as most of them were well aged by the time I was born.

This fact contributed to an early and almost regular encounter with death. The most severe being my own dad.

Mom was the "baby" of the family. She had always been kept in a 'cared for' position due to the grand mal seizures that besieged her from a very young age.

She was the daughter of William and Maria Baker, her dad being the son of William Twitty Baker, one of the only survivors of the Mountain Meadow Massacre, in which three generations of the Baker clan were slaughtered on September 11, 1857 on a Utah mountainside.

William and Maria Baker

The Baker clan was accustomed to tragedy and no doubt had found in their music the same happiness at some point in their past as I was just discovering and experiencing for the first time through their lives, instruments, and voices.

For some time during this, my early history, we lived in the parsonage of the old Lyman Mission Church. Living in this space was the result of the actions of the people of that church and community. The pastor and his wife, Brother and Sister Green, had a family too large for the small portion of the building that was set aside as housing. The church apparently took notice of our need and attempted to meet it.

Services at the old Lyman Mission were lively. Sunday nights were always preached by Sister Green, while Kenneth did the morning services. Sister Green preached like a fire storm, with intensity, passion and a lot of heart. Brother Green was more reserved, though it was evident that he believed what he was preaching as well.

Song services were many times simply ordered by "request." The leader would ask, "Does anyone have a song they would like to sing?" Anticipating the opportunity I would have already found the page; my hand would shoot up and I would give them the number. They were typically up-tempo and maybe something that would be considered a "camp" song. I would sing them mostly at the top of my lungs.

During the song service there were "specials" that were not really planned or announced ahead of time nor were there bulletins or computers and printers to create them. One regular participant was an older gentleman, Brother Hitson, who usually packed a harmonica in the pocket of his Hickory shirt. He was a tall lanky man.

I don't recall if he was asked to stand and share or if he would simply stand and say "I'd like to share." What I do recall clearly is that hymns sounded so much sweeter when Brother Hitson played them on his harmonica.

Singing hymns was a wonderful experience. Not only were they full of truth but they were also a first look at notes and timing signatures, bars and measures, bringing some form and structure to what I only knew as sound. But more than anything else, they would lift the spirits.

That music, the lyrics and the people who brought it all together, were probably the most influential of my entire life. I still have favorites which I learned while attending those services at the old mission.

It was a mixture of the music and the powerful word spoken during the evening services that drove me to find a place on my knees up front, where I would leave a puddle of tears in the old cupped wooden seats that were interconnected with rod iron.

Fifty years later, I see those times as the bedrock to my encounters with God. And I find it quite extraordinary that no matter the religion, or the maze one has to feel his or her way through, it is the heart that cries out to God that will find Him. He will always answer that cry.

# New Sounds

After a few years of living in that old parsonage, things changed. A new family moved into town, not only a family but a way of believing, a new way of worshiping, a new way of singing. The family was led by a very young, charismatic, and good looking man, Vernon Ketz.

We soon moved from the old parsonage to a home near the new Foursquare church in Burlington. Some of the music was the same but for the most part completely different. Most of which was led by Vernon, using an electric guitar with his wife Pearl, on the piano.

At that time and place electric guitars were held out as tools of the devil by the leaders of most churches. If that was the case then Vernon was leading, using Satan's tools, teaching the mysteries of God.

The evening services were also more up tempo, designed by nature to enhance the total "God" experience.

Traded, were tears for tears. I was still very young, probably around ten years of age. The times at the altar became more of a time of sadness, wondering why God would not give to me the "gifts" that the adults seemed so intent that I have.

It was more of the same thing that I had experienced in other areas of my life: there were the "haves" and the "have nots"; I just happened to fall into the camp of the latter.

Each Sunday night seemed only to repeat the previous one and served only to point to my deep need to have "the gifts" that were only transferred through the "laying on of hands" of the elders. This all continued until one Sunday night while standing down at the altar, I was emotionally drained, my arms were held up by others because I could no longer keep them in that position with my own strength. Tears were streaming down my face as I said "hallelujah" over and over again until it became inaudible and my tired speech began slurring, a mixture of water, sound, and emotion… Hallelujah, allelujah, elujah, lujuah, then, it was declared, "there, that's it…. that's it, you've got it!" Ah finally.

I am certain that the pianist was glad as she could now take a break.

For we (the pastor's daughter, Esther, was also a "seeker" of the most sacred of gifts) had finally received the promised Holy Spirit, which was evidenced through this new language that God had just given to us, also known as "tongues."

I was taught to practice this new language and it was not for me to understand what I was speaking; my duty was simply to let it flow, just kind of open your mouth and let your mind go. This is how we were taught that our faith would be increased. Ok. This was also a direct sign from God that you were now saved, you were guaranteed to "not burn in hell."

I have participated in various church groups, i.e., different organizations, or denominations. I am not going to comment on the silly stuff we were taught. You, as a reader, will just have to follow along on this little journey that I've been on. I'm most certain you will see how my own faith in God has grown despite some teachings that are purely religious and not Spirit-born.

One of the other gifts that was also administered through the "laying on of the hands" was one of deliverance. I witnessed firsthand the use of this, as it was used many times when mom would collapse in a seizure in the middle of the service. Those that had the "power" to heal would come rushing over and lay hands on her, they would begin speaking in tongues and try to cast out the demons that were in her, evidenced by the seizure. And so while mom convulsed into a tight knot of human flesh and bones, while blood would pour from her mouth as she always bit through her tongue, these folks would be reaching over the back of the pew or from the front trying to get their hands on her so they could put an end to her madness.

Their power must have been down just a little bit as the apparent fix only lasted until the next seizure when the demons got back in there and caused another takedown of Mom.

I am not certain how often this happened but it seemed as though it was every other day, which I am certain was not the case. However they were frequent and many were the times that the three of us were left to care for her. My younger sister also suffered with seizures; dealing with it was a daily part of our lives.

Where that power was maybe a little weak in Vernon, it was made up for in his musical abilities. Many times, while leading the song service, Vernon would literally jump up and over the altar, landing down front without missing a proverbial beat. He was a great guitar player and quite a showman.

When Mom was 7 weeks old, her mother was rocking her on the front porch. Apparently the rocker crept a little and both of them went tumbling down. Mom landed on an old rusty saw and it took a long time for her to heal. She had seizures all her life after that incident, up until 1975 when they stopped. Mom attributed them stopping to visiting a chiropractor. Maybe it wasn't demon possession at all but simply an ailment.

After a few years, Vernon took his family and returned to California. We were now removed from those who really cared for us and just seemed to exist on our own for a period of time.

# 1604 Township Street

Not long on our own and my Uncle Roy and Aunt T bought a second home, into which we moved. It's the only address that I can actually remember.

It was a small house and until the garage was remodeled into a bedroom, I slept on the back porch where the washer and dryer were located.

This really began a time of awareness of my family's poverty. It was hard to overlook things like pushing a shopping cart from town to our house; Mom with the three of us in tow, pushing that cart past the homes of all the other kids in town.

I was now at an age that I could really help. I began a paper route, and always gave a portion of my earnings to Mom to help with grub.

This was also a time of great fun as I began finding some independence and freedom. The paper routes gave me a lot of opportunity to roam around. I would wear a bike out every couple of years. I recall the first bike I bought on my own. I needed it, along with a set of baskets, to deliver all those papers around town.

There was a Coast To Coast store up town; the owners name was George. I was in the 5th grade when I started my first paper route. I approached George, and asked him if I could buy a bike on time, giving him a portion of each month's pay. He agreed. For decades following that time, I always felt as though he treated me with dignity and respect and I was grateful. I would shop at his store first when there was something I needed.

That little red house on Township Street provided stability that we never had before. The rent remained at a place that Mom could afford on the small disability she received. Therefore we stayed in that house for a number of years.

Prior to that time I don't know that we had ever lived in one spot for more than a few months. To this day, I attribute the ability to pack well stems from learning the skill through first hand experience.

It was typically Uncle Roy who would lend his truck and day to the process of moving us from one house to another. More than likely this single fact swayed any reluctance they may have had to take on a second home.

Schools were nearby, within walking distance, as were stores, thrift shops, and most anything we could want.

Several years in the same spot provided time to develop friendships. One of my close friends, Bruce, just lived a few blocks away. His Mom, like mine, was single and he too had a lot of responsibilities at home. But we enjoyed each other's company.

My first real stab at being a real musician came in the 5th grade when I entered band as a trumpet player. Bruce began playing the French Horn.

The bugle was always a haunting instrument for me. My first experience with it was listening to taps being played at Dad's full military funeral. One of the first things I learned to play was taps. Being in band, I learned that there was more than just sadness in horns.

I recall "Herb Albert and the Tijuana Brass," the albums that I picked up, the horns were just nuts. They would cut through a mix like no other instrument. I loved playing the trumpet.

I worked my way up to being "first chair" and held that position for some time. I was challenged by those who sat next to me, who wanted my position. While I played all the tunes in the band room that were required, at home I was on a mission of my own. The challenges came in the way of scales, something I did not study or try to excel in.

My older sister, Tricia, was listening to music by The Beatles, Led Zeppelin, Three Dog Night, The Bee Gees, Cream, Steppenwolf, etc... I would use money from my paper route to buy music books that held the secrets to playing these unbelievable melodies.

Looking back, I think playing second and third chair caused me to lose a little of the energy I started with. I still admired great horn players but a new instrument came onto my horizon: the guitar.

Moving back to Sedro-Woolley had also brought us back together with our old church family in Lyman. I would play specials on my trumpet. I remember my mom being so proud, as I stood before that small congregation and played Amazing Grace on my horn.

My first acoustic guitar came to me at a much greater cost than certain adults in my life could swallow. I had traded my ten-speed bike for it. I recall the "stick on flower" on the front of it, it was a "peace" guitar. My girl friend's father actually took it back to the pawn shop owner and retrieved my bike, which was probably worth ten times that of the guitar. It would be some time before I had another one in my possession.

Fond memories of this time in my life come from many places, and people, but one of my favorites is still of my dog, Sarge.

Sarge and Lonnie

Sarge was like no other dog. He would walk to school with me and hang out in the field until recess and lunch times. I could see him from my desk; he was sitting, as he did with his front paws crossed, out in the field. He would hang all day until school was out and then he would walk back home with me. He was my best friend.

He was a beautiful dog, part Samoa, part Collie, and part Shepherd. He spent his life with me, until I lost touch with him in Marblemount. More on that later.

He had a long mane, as if he was part lion. He wore it like a necklace. Everywhere we went people would comment on Sarge. Many times, we were asked if we would sell him or if he needed a good home. I was aware that my dog was beautiful. I have regrets though. I remember having to tie him up. I would never do that again.

One summer, while staying out on the "Good" family farm on Fir Island, he was hit by a truck. All four of his legs were broken and there was a large gash in the top of his head. He was completely immobile. I was told we needed to put him down but I would not hear of it.

We placed him on an old wooden sled and would pack him into the big old barn during the day, to keep him out of the sun, and then bring him out near the house, placing him under an old wagon in the evenings.

I will never forget the day, maybe a month or two after the incident, it was time to move him out of the barn when I looked out and saw him there under the wagon. He knew it was time to change his place and he was able to drag himself out there. He made a full recovery with only the dip in his head to remind us of the miracle of his healing.

Another favorite thing to do while living in Sedro-Woolley was to walk all the way up Township Street, to Hwy 20, early in the morning, where Uncle Roy would pick me up in his logging truck and I would ride with him to the log yards and back into the mountains to fetch another load.

Uncle Roy in one of his early logging trucks

Standing next to his truck, eye level was about the bottom of the door that I had to climb up into. This was before seat belt laws, and I mostly stood so I could see over the dash board.

I got to spend a lot of time with my Uncle Roy in that truck. I learned a lot about that man as he gave his time and most of his lunch to me.

Uncle Roy was at my Grandpa Baker's bedside when Grandpa died. Grandpa asked him to "watch out after Eva and the kids." He said that he would; that was a promise well kept.

One night we heard someone prowling around the house. We called the local police and Uncle Roy. Even though he lived in the next town Uncle Roy, was the one who arrived first.

While our little place on Township Street seemed stable, there was a cost being incurred that I knew little of. Having lived the entirety of her life under the watchful eye of her siblings, Mom wanted out from under the scrutiny of her older sister.

# Marblemount

We moved to Marblemount. We could have moved to the moon without much more change. The landscape was completely foreign to me. I knew no one. I missed my friends. And communication with our former world was very restricted.

The first year we lived in Marblemount the snow was 4 feet deep. It was cold but we were able to heat the little rental with an old pot belly stove. It was one of those very thin units, which once heated up would glow red. They were usually only good for maybe one season as they would literally burn up.

Uptown Marblemount consisted of a post office, one small grocery store and a gas station. The total population of the greater area was around 200, give or take a few.

I have to hand it to my Mom; I don't know how she did it but she bought me a motorcycle. It was a Kawasaki 90.

One thing that Marblemount provided was endless logging roads, all of which were easily accessible. I found great joy in riding into the surrounding mountains. When I would reach the end of the road or mountain top I would shut the bike down and just sit and listen to the quiet, looking down into the valley below.

I could spend days on end exploring. With this new ability to propel myself up or down the road, came also a sense of freedom. Even though I did not have a license, I rode on the highways to reach my "off road" destinations. There was little visible law enforcement, therefore very little fear of being "caught." Every one knew that there was only one State Trooper and he was stationed in Newhalem. If he had already been into town and was seen heading east, it pretty much meant we had the roads to ourselves.

# The Cascade River

The Cascade River will go down in my record books as one of the most beautiful places on earth.

It provided years of peace and safety in my life. I loved spending time exploring unknown portions of its wet, sometimes unreachable shoreline and sacred fishing holes rather than, say, going to school.

Many times I would meet the bus coming across the Skagit River bridge, with pole and creel in hand; I was heading the opposite direction. I would raise a hand to a few of my friends with a smile on my face.

I much preferred the solitude, the mountains and the river than all the drama that filled the classrooms and the hallways of the school.

Even prior to Mom moving us up to Marblemount I remember being somewhat of a loner. I recall that I would walk to school, past no less than three bus stops, where there was a line of kids waiting. I had been on a school bus and I didn't much care for the crowded seats and all the unknown kids. Mean kids had a way of pointing out what was already evident. So I would walk.

But once we moved to Marblemount things changed, I could no longer walk to school, because it was 20 miles down river. My first day in Concrete High School pretty much set my course for the next couple of very rocky years. The only friends I had were some of the toughest in the school so I guess I tried to align myself with them from the very beginning, trying to fit in.

First class, first day, first response; the first period teacher pointed me out as a new student and asked me a question. She said, "Lonnie, what does your dad do?" I responded, "He lies in his grave." Her reaction to my answer surprised me just as much as hearing those words leave my lips. She was so rattled that she left the room screaming.

That pretty much wiped out my chances of being a good kid at that point. But for the next several years I did attempt to do the normal school thing but there was no part of it that appealed to me. And my buddies loved the response as well, especially knowing they were not going to be in trouble for it.

I did make a few good friends which made school bearable until I was either kicked out or quit, both of which happened often until it made no good sense to continue wasting my time there.

The Cascade River was my refuge. I spent the next few years exploring as far as I could walk, and sometimes crawl along the banks of this glacier-fed tributary of the mighty Skagit.

Learning to catch the trout and white fish that lived in that river took some time. One local family that we came to know quite well was the Binchus family. They were known as "tar heels"; they had their roots in the Carolinas. There were many "tar heels" living in the upper Skagit Valley. I think they must have migrated out this way looking for work during the Great Depression.

Jim Binchus was my age and we had a mutual connection through his uncle Theo, who was probably the reason that Mom decided to move to Marblemount in the fist place. Theo just lived a few blocks from us in Sedro-Woolley, until he moved to Marblemount to help care for his Mom.

Jim had been raised there on the banks of the Cascade; he held the secrets to catching those fish. When I first began fishing with him, there was a lot of laughing. I could stand right next to him, using the exact same type of pole, reel, and even bait and yet how to hook those fish would elude me.

But given some time and experience, I learned. Here is the secret. One must hold the pole with one hand and then take hold of the line where it first leaves the reel. Hold the line gently with the thumb and index finger. You will "feel" the fish nibbling on the bait long before there is any indication given through the tip of the pole being disturbed. Once mastered, this very delicate technique would yield a stick full of fish, which were always welcomed back home.

The other fishing instructor who came into my life was our landlord, Ed Stafford. Ed and his wife Erma were also tar heels. Ed had carved out a very good living working in the woods. He had a few houses that he rented out, one of which was our home.

For whatever reason, Ed chose to reach out to me. He was probably in his late 60's or early 70's when we first moved to Marblemount. The difference in our ages seemed only to strengthen our friendship.

Ed had one passion in life, other than his wife Erma, Ed lived to fly fish. His fly of choice was always the "Royal Coachman Bucktail."

It was Ed who introduced me to the "hidden" fishing holes in the upper Cascade River. He taught me how to cast a line, not just from a river bank, but from a bank that had no room for the back cast, how to ford the river, read the water and know where the fish were waiting.

Ed was a small man, no taller than five feet and six or seven inches. Yet he could ford the Cascade River at some of the most treacherous places, with the help of a stick and the indoor-outdoor carpet that he glued to the bottom of his hip waders. I would not follow him... not at that time.

He would find a stick along the bank and break it off to be just long enough that it would fit under his arm pit.

There were what he called "virgin" fishing holes over on the other side, where there was no access. No one had been there. He would step into the water and prop that stick under his arm and begin, step by step, to inch his way across that very fast and sometimes furious water. The rushing water would pile up against him but each step was sure and in a few minutes he would be standing on top of some boulder, casting that Royal Coachman Bucktail.

Just before the fly was swept over the rocks into the next hole, a very fast trout would rise from the back portion of that hole and grab it... the fight was on! Ed had already begun taking up the slack as he saw it coming, which was equally as astounding as he only had one eye; the other had been kicked out by a horse when he was much younger. He would laugh out loud as the trout bent the pole and fought for all he was worth.

Ed always had his limit long before me, but he would help me fill my creel before we would begin the walk back up the steep terrain where the truck was parked alongside the old logging road.

Our trips to the upper Cascade were not the only fishing trips we took together. Ed had a motor home that he used to travel to his other fishing holes in Canada, and Eastern Washington, Montana, Idaho and other places where he knew the waters well.

He took me along on some of these trips, once to Canada to Loon Lake and several times to the east side of the state where he taught me other methods of fishing with both dry flies and wet flies, sinking and floating line, and using the fly rod with bait as well.

There was one small lake, not far from Marblemount, called Lost Lake. It only takes one trip into the lake to understand the name. It was more of a glorified bog on the lower section, but up behind the beaver dam, that was the "Grand Coulee" of beaver dams, was the good fishing holes.

We would find our way up and over the massive pile of debris that made up, what had to be the longest and highest beaver dam I have ever seen to this day. Once on the other side of that we would find our way along the bank, which was marshy, wet, and soggy, to a place where the water was deep. The only way to get out to the water was to get on one of the islands that were created from logs and moss.

The moss island was just a little dicey. There were holes where moss had not covered the water below. It was like peering down into a well while knowing that the only thing that kept you from sinking down into it was just green mushy stuff.

The moss was a foot or two thick and was draped across logs, twigs, sticks, and had formed these incredible floating islands.

There was only one way out to moss island. It was a pole that was probably felled by a beaver. It was not very big, maybe eight inches on the big side, which is where you would first step. Then it tapered down to a three or four inch diameter. This made the trek quite an adventure. There were no hand rails installed. There was nothing to hang onto.

The one thing that always bothered me was that this pole was submerged beneath the water, at the deepest point it was probably six inches under. It was skinny and it was slick. But when you take into consideration the unfished waters that lay just beyond that little deterrent, there was no questioning the benefits outweighed the chances and risks. I never fell in while making the trek out to the island.

Once there we tossed our flies out onto the water, which was clear as glass. You could see the cutthroat coming up from the deep long before they grabbed the fly.

We would fill up our creels and find our way back across that skinny little pole. Fishing with Ed was always an adventure.

The Cascade River area was also a gathering place for many of the "hippies" that had found their way there in the late sixties and early seventies. It was also home to Jim Clark, the reddest of red necks. Many days would find me cutting across the south end of his property to a place where I could ford the Cascade, which saved me about a mile of walking to reach one of my favorite spots on the bank of that river.

Hippies were "the scourge" of Marblemount and any other place that they chose to reside, if you were to believe what the other locals had to say about them. Maybe it was their way of looking down at them that really made me want to get to know them. Maybe it was the way I felt about myself and how I had come to realize that others looked at me as something "less than." For whatever reason, I found myself being drawn to find out for myself who these "hippies" really were.

It was easy to spot one of them, as they dressed different than the locals. And their hair was always a dead giveaway. Maybe it was the fact that they did dress different, yes, maybe that was it. I knew how it felt to dress different. I think it was this difference that helped me walk past three bus stops on my way to school. My clothes were always different. Well, not so much different as simply older.

Growing up, Mom would take us to thrift shops to find us "new clothes." We would dig through boxes of shoes to find footwear, shoes that one of the other kids in town had the privilege of breaking in for us. The hippies had shoes like that too. And the clothes they wore certainly did not come off a designer rack. Their clothes were usually functional for what they needed to be. If they were too long they would be rolled up. If they were too loose they would have suspenders to help hold them in place. If their pants were too short they could add a hem to the bottom, which could also be tailored to "flare" out a bit.

It was easy to get to know them, and they were very accepting of me, for who I was. They didn't look down on me. They also had rules, which were communicated in a fashion.

I recall first coming into one camp, where a guy and his lady were living in a plastic shelter. His lady was absolutely stunning, beautiful. I must have been admiring her beauty a little too much; he caught my eye and slapped one hand down onto his hip where his knife was in a sheath. He didn't say anything but I got the message. I could enjoy the fire, have some coffee, and sit a spell, but that lady was off limits. I got it.

I never had any confrontations with any hippie at any time. However, I cannot say the same for time I spent as a redneck. But that comes later... let's just live in Marblemount as the youngest hippie for a while.

# Hippie

During those few years of attempting school, my hair began to grow and I didn't see any reason to stop it from doing just that. Somewhere in that time someone called me a hippie and it stuck. That was my name. I accepted it gladly as I had come to find that being a hippie was a good thing, or at least different. And most hippies could play a guitar and shake a song out of their shirtsleeve at the drop of a hat, or head band.

Head bands were actually a very functional piece of clothing. When your hair is long, it's a way to keep it out of your eyes, to hold your hair in place without the use of chemical hairspray or sticky goo.

I loved guitars, loved the sounds they made. And I loved the freedom that I enjoyed while sitting and listening to one of those hippies play and sing.

As I found my way deeper into that little subculture, I also found music that I had never heard. It was different from what was played on the radio, or at least what little bit I had experienced. It was over on Clark Road, at Roger and Patty's place where I first heard Jesse Colin Young sing, "Wings Of A Dove." The old house they lived in wasn't much. There were boxes used for end tables, old rugs covered the wobbly floor, and kerosene lanterns for light, but that music was from heaven.

One of my early mentors on the guitar was Greg Hethorn. Greg had an old flattop Gibson that he would let me play. It looked like it was falling apart, the finish was all cracked and coming off but the sound that came out of that thing would make me want to melt into a heap in the middle of the floor and just listen.

The deep, rich tones could be felt when he played it and the way he played it was different as well. He would do hammer on's and pull offs before I even knew what that meant. It was mesmerizing to watch, and wonderful to hear. And then he would show me how to do it.

Eating with hippies was always a humble experience. There was not "plenty." Meals were always home cooked soups and garden vegetables and dried goods. Even though there was not an abundance of food, I was always welcome at their table.

I found a lot of false perceptions regarding hippies, one of which was their work ethic. They worked just as hard as anybody else. Typically it was jobs that others did not want like "planting trees."

And fire fighting seemed to be a favorite and one in which I shared their experience - well, until it was found that I was only 16, at which time I was put in a small plane and flown home.

# Walking

Mom must have missed her down river friends, as she would sometimes leave to visit and not return for a number of days, or a week or two. By then I was old enough to take care of myself, which I did pretty much from around fifteen on.

I too, had friends that I left behind, down river. The one most influential in my endless hitch hiking journeys down hwy 20 was Terry, a girl friend of mine.

Terry lived up on Dukes Hill just north of Sedro-Woolley. Initially I liked her sister, Vickie, but Terry took a liking to me and was pretty straight up about how she felt about me. I guess they agreed to share me as we were all good friends for a long time.

Their Mom also liked me and I got along with her well. But when I decided that Terry would be my girl and not Vickie, well, she sat me down and said, "listen, buddy, these are my girls and you're not going to be messing with their emotions…. You make up your mind who you like." So I cleared up any confusion and stuck with my decision.

The only thing that kept us apart was the long 50 miles between our homes and I had no way of getting there unless it was on my thumb.

Over the next few years, I walked. I walked a lot. I don't know how many times I covered those miles, but I know it was many. The one thing I didn't believe was right, was to just stand there and ask for a ride. So I walked. I would raise my thumb when a car came up behind me, but it didn't matter if they stopped. I would walk all the way if I had too.

Walking became a way of life and one that I have never regretted. Walking was healthy and gave me a lot of time to think.

As I became more and more integrated with Terry's family, I began working for her dad in the summer months. He had a small business installing septic systems and working with equipment.

Vickie began seeing another guy who became my best friend. His name was Mick.

Mick and I would walk down the hill toward town together after visiting the sisters. We would sing at the top of our lungs, recanting the words of the Eagles song, "Take It Easy."

We were all making big plans; we were going to have a double wedding. However Terry and I broke up. Mick and Vickie did go on to wed. Not long after that, Mick took his own life. Mick and I were close. That loss hit hard. I still love him.

# Wind River

After Terry and I broke up there was no longer a need to travel down river. It gave me a lot more time to just be. Being a hippie was more than a label at this point; I had found new friends that were really like my family.

The hippies had formed a "Hot Shot" team, firefighters that would be transported around to fight some of the worst fires. They were very proud of their reputation and wanted to include me. There were oversights made by some on my behalf, I am most certain.

There was one fire over on the Olympic Peninsula. Bags were packed, the bus was loaded and we were off. I had never been part of something so grand. There were about 40 of us on that bus.

One of our stops was at a Denny's restaurant. It's quite a sight to see 40 hippies swarm into a well known, downtown eatery. Some of the local patrons were a little nervous, which always gave us a good laugh. We were harmless.

Once we reached our destination, Wind River Ranger Station, eating was more in line with the profession, being served outside and in tents.

This is where we received our paper sleeping bags, something that I had only heard of prior to this. They were like textured cardboard that was sewn together on the sides. It makes me laugh now but at the time it was pretty cool.

During the day we would go "put out smokes" and during the night we would all gather around in one of the big old log buildings at the heart of the ranger station.

They circled up in the middle of that big old building, using chairs and whatever could be found to sit on, and it began. There was one guitar. I am most certain it was Greg's old flat top Gibson. It was passed around this circle of friends, each person taking a turn at playing a song.

The mood was peaceful, everyone seemed to be in the same frame of mind, the old Gibson let go of those wonderful tones that were stored inside, an endless well of harmonics, notes, and melodies. I was in heaven.

I sat off to one side, being the youngest and just taking it all in. I am most certain that the pot we had shared was contributing to the experience, but even to this day I have only wonderful memories of sharing that time with those hippies at Wind River.

The next day, at the bottom of one very black and smoky ravine, I got a message. I was wanted up on top. So with bladder bag and pulaski in hand, I climbed up and out of the ravine to the waiting truck. They took me back to the ranger station and then off to the local airport to a waiting Cessna. They flew me back to Concrete airport where another worker was waiting to drive me home.

The flight home was a real treat for me. I thoroughly enjoyed peering down over the Puget Sound, Seattle, and looking ahead and seeing the mountains that made the Skagit Valley that had always been my home.

The discovery of my underage status and the plane ride home never would have happened were it not for a call from a friend of mine, Diane. She had moved into an apartment next to my home. She had "come out" of the hippie scene and was trying to keep me from what she saw as a very bad thing.

She had been frequenting a Christian coffee house all the way down in Mount Vernon. She wanted me to go down valley with her; she wanted to take me to that coffee house. She was a few years older than I but had really taken a liking to me. She was persistent but I was stubborn. I didn't go with her soon.

Even though I had been portraying the "tough guy" image with my Vibram sole boots, buck knife, scruffy face and suspenders, and Top tobacco in the pocket of my Hickory shirt, she saw through me and mostly laughed at my exterior. I liked her and it was easy to let her see my heart.

It was also easy to be a hippie; it seemed more natural than anything else. But I decided there was no "future" in that life style. I went to my sister's house and had her cut off all my hair. And in a matter of days I took a job with one of the local loggers working in the woods.

The hippies had their pot, which was said to be the gateway to being a heroin addict and worse, but the loggers had hard liquor and lots and lots of beer. Though I can recount multiple encounters with pot, I do not recall ever seeing the death and destruction I found associated with alcohol. Hard liquor left people dead alongside the roads and in their homes; the worst effects of pot were the munchies.

There is no secret that working in the woods is one of the most dangerous occupations in the world. But I think coupled to that are so many tragic accidents that could have been prevented by simply going home after work and resting instead of the local tavern and drinking the night away, which is what most of the crew did.

Still too young to really be put in harm's way, I spent a lot of time building fire trail, with some limited exposure to choker setting and working as a chaser on the landing, both of which were very, very dangerous places to be.

# The East Side

My older sister had married when she was 17. Her and Hans were several years into their life together. They had decided to move to Soap Lake. Mom and Cheryl, my younger sister, were going to move there as well.

Even though I had been on my own for the most part, I was still under Mom's roof, even if it was only once or twice a month, so it was off to the east side of the state.

It was a full load. I recall Danny Green and I in the back of the U Haul, doing everything we could to stop the load from creeping out the door, which was left half open.

I'm not sure what prompted our move to the east side, other than Tricia wanting to keep track of Mom, even if it meant moving her to the other side of the mountains. Tricia really had the place of matriarch, and felt responsible for the care of the family.

I lived with Hans and Tricia, which was a combustible mix. Hans and I did not get along well. However, we had one thing in common, electric guitars - loud electric guitars.

My stay on the east side was a short one. I had gained employment down in Moses Lake, where I was working a night shift putting potato harvesters together. I had received a ride back into Ephrata where Hans had agreed to pick me up, as he had kept my car the night before. He never showed. It was the middle of winter, solid ice and compacted snow on the ground with the wind blowing hard, stripping away any heat from my unprotected body.

The four-mile walk to Soap Lake in that blistering cold was all I needed to decide that I was going back to the west side of the mountains, whether or not I had any place there to live.

I think I hung out with Danny for a few days, where he lived in Marysville with his mom. It didn't take long for the two of us to find ourselves headed up to Skagit County. I guess we were both going back to what was familiar. It didn't take long for reality to set in.

# Life On The Ranch

I never owned a horse or had a place for one prior to my stay on Jim Clark's Dude Ranch. 1974 marked the beginning of a new time in my life. It was the first time that I experienced living in the same home with a man at the helm.

The circumstances that paved my way to that wonderful place on earth on the bank of the Skagit River in Marblemount were, well, let's just say "a little precarious" to say the least.

I had been incarcerated in juvenile detention due to forgery. Danny Green and I had been living in his car and were simply getting hungry so we wrote ourselves a check and claimed we had done some work for our old school bus driver. It worked once so we did it twice. We were not hard to find. Everyone knew where we parked alongside the highway in Birdsview, where we slept at night. When the first check cleared, they came and arrested Danny. I knew that tomorrow they would come for me, so I waited.

I was arrested and placed in custody the following day, where I didn't have to worry about what to eat, where to sleep or how I would bath. They gave me three meals a day, a bed, and allowed me to shower each day as well.

I am not sure how it came about or why Jim offered his home to me. I think it may have been my aunt Darlene, who was a half sister of my dad, who may have begun the negotiations…, that's just a hunch. Jim had been married to her previously.

When I was given the options of either returning to live with Mom in Eastern Washington or accept Jim's offer, the choice was easy. I had been living in a car. I was not going back to eastern Washington - not at this time anyway.

So I found myself face to face with the one man of whom so much was spoken, Jim Clark. I had been to his home before but never to his knowledge, as were other teenagers when Jim and Cary were out of town. His daughters, Cindi and Deb, were fun to hang out with - but only when

Jim was away.

This was also the man that I was told shot my beloved Sarge, while I was on a trip down river. I was told that Sarge had taken to chasing deer and the neighbor called Jim to come and take care of the problem.

He was the "Red" in redneck and the "Hard" in hard work. He was all bull, as in just as strong as any and known to use horns if needed. My time with him started in the kitchen where he laid out the rules. He had me take a seat at the kitchen table and began. He said I could ride his horses, drive his tractor, shoot his guns, and sleep in my own bed but never in his. He asked me if I understood, to which I responded in the affirmative.

I had never eaten as good in all of my life nor had I ever worked as hard. He would wake me prior to the sun rising and I would begin my chores, which included milking several cows by hand, feeding calves. Then I would come in for breakfast, which was usually steak and eggs, potatoes, fresh milk, biscuits with gravy or homemade butter. Then I would head back out to the barn yard to clean stalls, care for livestock, build fence, put up hay or whatever was needed to be done.

I don't really remember lunches being a big deal but dinner was nothing short of incredible, meat and potatoes and lots of it. The only thing I remember them buying was sugar, salt, and flour, as they grew all their own food and put it up, canning most of it.

No one ever walked away from that table hungry. After dinner there were still projects that needed more tending. I would work until it was time to fall into bed. The next morning would start again. Jim would slide the door open on that little room out on the front porch where I slept, "Hey, kid, it's time to get up."

That was the place I slept until I moved out into the bunkhouse, which held men who came on in the summertime to help with contracts that Jim had acquired through the National Park Service for trail construction.

During these times my duties seemed to quadruple as I had my normal chores along with a regular ten or twelve hour day in the woods. I remember when we'd all get back to the ranch after a day in the mountains, the guys would settle in and relax for the evening and I would try to catch up on my normal duties. But the work outside the ranch provided me with real income, which was easily saved for the simple reason that I never left the ranch to spend any of it.

I don't really know when it became more like a home than a place to be but I remember when I was dubbed "the kid." Cary wrote it on the end of my lunch pail. I would see it every day as I grabbed it before jumping into one of his shiny, macho four-wheel-drive Fords. "The Kid"- that was my new identity.

The rest of the crew were mostly grown men, the exception being "cookie"- I don't remember her real name. She was hired on after Jim sent our first cook down the trail in the middle of the night after he laid him out in front of the tool tent, where Jim slept.

The cook had spent the evening down at the inspector's camp, where he had drunk a little wine instead of dealing with his duties. When he came back to camp Jim confronted him and the cook responded by saying something to Jim about a horse that he had found and tied to a hitching rail back at his place earlier that year.

The horse was from the ranch, which had gotten loose. He said, "This reminds me of a horse." You see, Jim saw his horse and took it. He didn't stop and ask questions or seek out who should receive a grand thank you; he just took his horse back home. Apparently he thought the cook said, "You look like a horse." So Jim knocked him out. Our new cook was much prettier and there were no more midnight confrontations.

Marblemount was a wonderful place, a strange mix of long-haired hippies and short-haired red necks. The two did not blend very well. A little piece of paradise (in the summer months) nestled in the foothills of the North Cascade Mountain Range. Shimmering, bubbling creeks emptied into the small but mighty Cascade River which dumped into the Skagit River just down on the south end of the property.

Jim was a very well known hunting guide. Jim and Cary would pack people into remote areas of the Cascades and would stay with them and help them find the beast they were hunting for.

I had never killed a deer prior to living on the ranch. My first season with Jim found me up on the big mountain that towered over the property. It was called B&W, named after the father and son who burned to death in the fire that consumed its steep west face, some years prior.

There was no threat of fire when we were on top searching for a buck. The snow was deep and it was cold, but I didn't notice. Jim had equipped me with a 30.06 Winchester bolt action rifle, which I held close to my body, one hand on the trigger the other supporting the weight of the barrel. We were working our way across the high face of the mountain. Jim was down below me, we were using one of his favorite ways of skirting a hillside on a hunt.

I heard him whistle, he pointed up the hill. There was a huge white tale buck. I took aim, pulled the trigger and the shot rang out across the white, chilly landscape. The deer fell immediately. I held the gun up over my head and let out a war hoop. Jim looked at me like I was just a little silly, but he seemed to understand the jubilation of my first kill.

Venison was typically mixed with beef, which we raised. So hunting season was always hand in hand with butchering. Mixing the venison with beef tamed the flavor a bit and made the beef stretch further than it would have otherwise.

The winter months passed quickly and soon the cycle of working in the hills returned. The next season was different, in that the work was located deep in the heart of the Cascades, and there were no roads into our location. My living situation had also changed. I had rented myself a little house in the town of Hamilton. But I was still working for Jim. I had to live with Jim until I was 18 at which time I was ready to try life on my own again.

Our transport began early in the morning, with a ride in the truck to Ross Dam, a mile hike down to the dam and a 10-mile ride up the lake, where we would begin our 17-mile hike into the back country work site.

My pack weighed in at about 80 lbs. We were all in top shape and made the hike in a matter of hours. We would stay in camp for 10 days and then come out for 3 days and then do it all over again.

We were building bridges by hand from native materials on sight. Each day was a challenge. Our crew consisted of from six to ten guys.

I worked hard for Jim, not because he demanded it but because of the gratitude that I felt in my heart. He opened his home to me and helped change my life. That was never a talk we had nor do I even know if he was ever aware of the transformation that took place because of his actions. He knew I worked hard for him and I knew that he appreciated it.

One morning I was working alone, close enough to some of the crew that we could hear each other, but alone. I was knocking knots off what would become a bull rail on a bridge we were constructing. The long pole was standing up against a tree to provide easy access to the knots.

I was using Jim's double bitted axe, something that I was warned "not" to do. Jim took great pride in keeping his tools sharp enough to shave with, something he had demonstrated to us one evening around the fire in camp. It was as sharp as a razor.

Wielding an axe was not something that I had learned growing up. I could make my way around a chopping block alright but this was more like surgery and I only knew how to apply band aids. That's a bad analogy but it will make sense here in a minute.

The mistake I made was standing on the same side of the pole from which I was removing the knots.

I raised that axe up over my head to apply a good amount of force at my target. I brought the axe down and missed slightly. The axe glanced off the pole and the force which I had applied pushed it all the way to the ground, which was being covered by my brand new pair of boots.

There was no stopping the axe. It sank deep into my foot. It felt as if it had traveled all the way through the bottom of the boot.

I reached down and grabbed the head of the axe and pulled. It came out nearly as smoothly as it had entered but when it came out so did a fountain of blood. My blood.

I yelled over to my comrade, "Rocky!", …….. "yeah," he replied. "I need some help!" He came over, took one look and headed off to find Jim.

By the time Jim was back with the crew I had found my way out to the trail. He unlaced by boot and gently pulled it off. When I was making my way out to the trail, it felt as if I'd chopped my toe off, so I was glad to see it was still attached, but it was floppy, I had cut the tendon. My foot was laid open like a fillet of salmon, sliced just as clean as any surgeon could have done. The axe had gone straight through, in between my second and third toe.

I wanted to cry, not because of the injury but because I felt like I had really let Jim down.

The inspector on the job with us had a radio that worked off repeaters in the mountains. It took a while to track him down and then a while longer to get a message out but eventually someone at the ranger station did relay the message that we needed a helicopter.

In the meantime they had to get me to a place where they could land. They packed me for a while and then put me in a wheelbarrow, in which I finished out the trip to the landing zone.

It was quite a few hours before help arrived. I was grateful when it did. They gave me a pain pill and stuck me in the back of that small chopper. They gave me a set of headphones, which I used to talk to the pilot.

Once down out of the mountains I gave him directions to United General Hospital. Apparently he wasn't from the area or had never taken anyone to emergency. I think he flew a lot of cedar for some of the area cutters.

The next time Jim and the crew came out he told me how much production had gone down. I did not wait for the stitches to be taken out, as a matter of fact Jim took them out for me.

Once back on the job site, the walk from camp to our work site caused my foot to bleed so I was given special treatment and was allowed to ride one of the draft horses that we used to pull logs. Come to think of it, I think that's how I got back to camp that time. The time before that I was flown in.

# Pitch Black Darkness

Have you ever noticed that we get what we need? I mean, all of us have lessons to learn and as the old adage goes, "When the student is ready the teacher appears."

One of the things I learned at a young age was fear. I think it stemmed from reaching into my dad's casket and touching his arm. I couldn't understand death. It was scary. Somehow, death and darkness got all wrapped up together. I had always been scared of the dark.

What propels us into our lessons? Well, for me, it was love - or at least the thought of love. This one particular three-day stretch off, I had decided to stay in and earn extra money along with Glen, one of the crew. So the crew took off and Glen and I stayed. It only took one day and I decided that I wanted to walk out and see my girl friend.

Glen kinda stoked the fire a bit. I think he was jealous of my relationship with Jim anyway and he knew this great idea of mine would not end well. We sat there in camp and talked about the walk out and discussed how long it would take to get down to the dam.

I decided that I was going to do it and threw my pack on and hit the trail at about 2:00 in the afternoon. I figured that I could probably sprint most of the way to the lake and then cross the dam and head up to the road in plenty of time to hitch a ride into town.

I did sprint, probably for the first ten miles or so. But the trip back was different than how we came in. My trip out would take me up and over a pass called Little Beaver. It was not a pass I was familiar with. I did not think about how steep that pass was nor how much it would slow me down.

When I made it to Little Beaver I still had some daylight but it was going fast. I had one small flashlight that only lasted a short time until I found myself in a dark that I had never experienced before. It was so dark that I could put my hand directly in front of my face and not even see a shape. By that time I had made it over the pass but my night was long but over. I kept walking. When my feet would leave the trail I would feel the brush and whatever lay along the path, and then I'd move back over and keep going, feeling my way.

That night I faced that demon we call fear. It came at me with all sorts of sights and sounds. I thought there were cougars, I thought there were bears, I thought too much but I just kept walking. I didn't have a lot of other choices.

It was well into the night before I reached Ross Lake. Once there I breathed a sigh of relief. As I broke out of the heavy forest I could make out shapes again and there were a few stars out. I could see the lake, and I was happy. There was a sign posted next to the trail at that point. Once up close I could make out the white lettering. It said, "Ross Dam - 6 miles" with an arrow pointing west.

I was not out of the woods yet but the stars in the sky did bring some relief from the pitch darkness I had traveled through. I made it to the dam and then started the mile ascent up to the highway. Once there I only wanted to get home. I thought maybe I could find some keys in one of the cars in the parking lot. I wasn't going to steal a car, just borrow it to get me home. I started prowling, searching for keys. A couple shots rang out from a nearby camper that I didn't see. That pretty much ended my search for an easy ride home. I started down the highway. Now, instead of trying to hitch a ride, each time a car appeared I hid, thinking whoever capped off those rounds near the parking lot could be looking for me.

I arrived at Thunder Creek Campground at about 5:00 a.m. I was tired, beat, and wanting to go home. I had traveled approximately 35 miles with a heavy back since 2:00 p.m. of the previous afternoon.

A camper came into the restroom to shave. I was sitting against the wall. My feet had blisters, my legs were sore and I knew that my actions were not good. We talked a bit; he asked me which way I was heading. He and his wife gave me a ride.

I called Jim that day and told him what I had done. He told me to be at the ranch first thing in the morning. I flew back into camp with the inspector, who was flown in from the ranger station at Marblemount.

I think Glen was surprised to see me. That was a great lesson, and I realized that dark was just that, dark. I lived, learned, and laughed about my silly decision. I did not see my girl friend that trip out.

I went on to work for Jim off and on for the next twenty years, always trying to repay the debt of gratitude that I felt toward him.

I could not say no to Jim. One day, after spending twelve hours in the cab of one of his dump trucks, my old back injury was really talking to me.

I needed to go home and recover from the day, but Jim was bucking bails, putting up alfalfa. I couldn't walk past.

I stopped and helped.

That was my last day driving truck and began another two years of being broken down because of my back injury.

# Short Stay At Bible Way

Prior to my short stint on the east side of the state and subsequent living arrangements on the ranch, I had joined Diane in a trip to Mount Vernon to what had then become a church, Bible Way.

Though my initial association with that group was superficial and brief, it was a connection to something I missed. I knew they were genuine and a time came when I was ready to try to get down to the business of getting my life on track again.

One night I was cruising on my chopper, a 650 BSA with raked forks and hard tail suspension. The bike was cool, but I was not. I realized that I was deeply lonely and I wanted to refocus, to once again seek after God. I called Greg, and he came and met me for coffee.

Greg offered me a place to stay, and an opportunity to hang out in a safe haven. There would be rules and work, both of which I needed.

This connection with people who wanted to live a life that pleased God, was a good one. They taught accountability and a departure from drugs and alcohol. They were genuinely happy people and the music they played and sang was a new flavor that I had not previously experienced.

It was a time when contemporary Christian music had come onto the horizon. People like Larry Norman, with "I wish we'd all been ready," and Randy Stonehill were singing about God in a way that was fresh and new.

Though my stay with at Bible Way was short, there was one incident that happened while there that will never be forgotten.

One Sunday I joined a friend, Matt, as he was riding along with his friend to pick up someone from the airport. There were two cars traveling together on our way to Seattle. Candy was driving the old Plymouth station wagon in which she, Matt, and I were riding.

We were speeding, really speeding. I was compelled to offer a silent prayer, asking God to protect us. Seconds later Candy lost control of the car and we began fishtailing back and forth across those three or four lanes of blacktop. I was sitting in the middle and glanced over at the speedometer. We were doing 95 mph when we left the pavement and were launched high into the air.

Witnesses told me later what happened. We hit a curb, which sent the big car end over end, landing on its top in the median at which point the force caused the car to tumble sideways, rolling over and over again until it came to rest on its side, with me sitting next to it. It was flatter than a fritter.

I looked up and saw Matt lying on the freeway. I guessed that he was dead, and I heard Candy screaming in the rig, saying, "get out of it, get out of it"

I jumped up and began running down the median, as far away from the car as I could get.

What went unseen, except to me, was the hand of God answering the prayer that I had whispered seconds before the crash. Here's where it gets tricky, trying to put into words what I experienced.

You know those little fiber optic lights that were so popular during the 70's? Someone had figured out how to make lamps by bending light, which would follow those strands of fiber out to the end where there would be a little "dot" of light. It's that little dot that I want to focus on.

Take that dot and multiply it by, oh say, a billion. Now surround yourself with all those dots of light. Put them all right against your body. Let those billion dots of light support you, carry you if you will. Each dot is a different color and each one is holding you up and away from any harm.

That was my experience. God carried me through that wreck and continued holding me as I was ejected through one tiny hole, and landed outside of the car on my butt. One more role and I would have been as flat as that old station wagon was.

I was not totally unscathed; I had bit a hole in my lip and broken a bone in my foot. As for Matt, he was fine except for a stomach ache and Candy had a scratch on her neck.

Even after such an experience, it seemed fairly easy to find my way back into the life style that I had been living.

I would go and visit my old friends; I would tell them of my new way of life, thinking that I could influence them. It would not be long before the joint that was being passed around would be found in my hand. What was one little toke… it wouldn't hurt. These were my friends.

After a few tokes, it probably wouldn't be all that bad to have just one beer. And so the decline had begun.

# Between a Boy and a Man

In between - it's a hard place to be. The one thing my grandfather said to me on Father's day, back in 1964, was this: "Son, you are the man of the house now. Your dad is not coming home. You need to take care of your mom and your sisters."

I had already had 12 years of being a man by the time I was eighteen. In my mind I was ready to be married and to take care of a family.

The night I met Mary Lynn was probably not one of my best moments. I had come from a small get-together, where a handful of us drained a keg. I was out driving around, alone.

I spotted Glen's jeep and chased him down. He pulled into one of those all night restaurants. He had two women with him. One he was dating, the other was alone.

They had just come from a bar, so we were all in the same state of mind. Conversation at the table was mostly about Glen and I and our experiences in the mountains together.

Mary Lynn was beautiful. I caught her looking at me in a way that cannot be denied.

When we left the restaurant, she wanted to ride in my 69 Chevelle. I obliged and drove her back to their car. She invited me over. Not long after we met, we moved in together.

Initially, I was happy to have found someone, as I had become entangled in an affair. I thought this was my way out. But this only complicated my life further, now including other lives as well.

Our two worlds collided and we tried for the next 14 years to make it work.

It seems like we spent the first two years in the bedroom, and when we came out we realized we didn't have much in common.

After living together for the first year, I told her that I could not live with her without being married. My heart was talking to me. I explained all that I knew of God and living in a way that honors Him.

The next day she left, I found a note that said, "Marry me or get out."

At that point I was deeply invested in the relationship. I wanted to do the right thing. Not long after that we were married. However the license was never filed with the court; it was someone's oversight and not something that I even knew until many years after our divorce.

We had two children together, Kari Lynn and Karisa Ann. We also raised a son from her previous marriage. His name is Eric.

When our world came crashing in, when it was evident that we were no longer going to be a couple, my heart took a hit that was probably worse than losing my dad.

I lost 30 pounds in two weeks and remained as skinny as a cheap rail fence for the next two years. It took another two decades to regain a sense of stability and a genuine relationship with a woman.

There were some interesting moments while we were still together. One of them happened on top of a mountain.

# Stripes Of The Fool

In the book of Proverbs there is a warning to all of us about the results of foolish choices. It states several times that there are stripes awaiting the back side of a fool.

I have always felt that my back injury was God's way of correcting me as my choices to be involved in an affair were obviously very foolish. I smashed several discs in my lower back which decommissioned me for many years. I still suffer with that injury and it still reminds me that I am loved. Now doesn't that sound strange?

You see, further reading in the Bible clearly teaches that God does discipline those that He loves. I know you can take this thought process and head a thousand different directions with it, but it is not my intent to make a statement for anyone other than myself.

That statement being that my actions were foolish and I have stripes on my back to prove it.

# Mountaintop Meeting

Mary Lynn and I had been married for about 5 years when I began driving truck for National Frozen Foods, hauling corn from the fields in eastern Washington to the cannery in Burlington.

I loved driving trucks; it was old brain for me. From the very first time I rode with Uncle Roy, I knew I wanted to drive big trucks.

I was on top of Snoqualmie Pass, checking my tires and brakes and getting ready to head down the pass.

We were permitted for oversized loads. Our rigs were like trains going down the highway, two trailers that measured out over 75 feet long. A typical load was about 105,000 lbs. Most 18 wheelers haul a max of 80,000 lbs.

That particular day was no different than many others; I had pulled over at the top of the pass and was checking my rig before heading down the mountain.

I had my little hammer in hand and was thumping my tires, checking for any that were low on air. There was a white El Camano that pulled off the highway and parked right in front of my rig. The guy rolled his window down and wanted to talk to me. I walked over to the rig and wondered if he wasn't having car problems as there was steam rolling out from under the hood.

He began speaking, he said, "God told me to stop and talk to you. I didn't want to because I'm in a hurry to get to Seattle where I am scheduled at a radio station. But He told me to stop."

Whozza!!!!! My mind was flipping out. Who in the world was this joker and what planet was he from? Maybe it was Satan himself, come to deceive me. All kinds of things went through my mind. But my heart, well, there was a different story echoing there.

It's an interesting place to be when your mind goes one way and your heart goes another.

The man beckoned me closer to the car. He asked if I was a Christian. What I wanted to say is not what came out. I wanted to say, "I might of been once, what's it to ya?" But I don't think I said a word. He beckoned me closer still and said "I want to read something to you." He read a passage from the Gospel of Matthew.

> "Therefore hear the parable of the sower: When anyone hears the word of the kingdom, and does not understand it, then the wicked one comes and snatches away what was sown in his heart. This is he who received seed by the wayside. But he who received the seed on stony places, this is he who hears the word and immediately receives it with joy; yet he has no root in himself, but endures only for a while. For when tribulation or persecution arises because of the word, immediately he stumbles. Now he who received seed among the thorns is he who hears the word, and the cares of this world and the deceitfulness of riches choke the word, and he becomes unfruitful. But he who received seed on the good ground is he who hears the word and understands it, who indeed bears fruit and produces: some a hundredfold, some sixty, some thirty."

Again, my mind was throwing up walls and doing everything it could to protect me from this strange invasion of my own personal space…. But my heart, it was crying.

Then this man wanted to pray with me. This all happened in a matter of minutes. As much as I wanted to resist praying, I knelt at his opened door, took his hand and prayed.

It had been a while since I really tried to seek the face of God. I was taught that if you were not living your life in a certain way that it would be better to "not" do anything toward God, which would leave all of us completely and utterly condemned. Fortunately, God seeks out those who are his, and does not stop reaching out based on our inability to maintain a perfect life.

I cried all the way down the mountain that day. And once home I explained to Mary Lynn all that had happened. I told her that we needed to be in church, that she needed to give her life to the Lord.

We began attending the Foursquare church that Vernon Ketz had planted many years before.

I will never forget what happened the first time I lifted my voice in a Sunday service. As we began singing, God whispered in my ear, "I missed your voice."

After some time of regular attendance and study, the pastor, Don Coulter, approached me and wanted me to lead the worship services. I thought he had the wrong guy and may have stated as much but he was persistent.

He was a good man and I loved him, the same way I loved Jim. I did as he requested, though it was probably one of the most uncomfortable things I had ever done. I was quiet and shy by nature, or by the circumstances that had formed me, and standing in front of a large congregation was a very big step. It was like getting on the bus instead of walking past the bus stop just because of my own perception of what others may be thinking about me.

The man's name that stopped on the top of that mountain was Tab Morgan. For many years I thought he was an angel as I could never find him. However, many years later and with a Google search I did find him.

I met with Tab and shared my testimony at one of his services. I found him to be a man like me, just a man, still seeking God.

Though we found some help for our troubled marriage, as Don and his wife Bev, would counsel us. And though we made some great friends while attending that church, we left it because I could no longer agree with all the doctrine.

The whole "tongues" teaching is a very deeply engrained part of that religion, and one that is not open for discussion. When one steps away from that bent, it's almost as if you have turned your back on God, and could be considered "apostate," completely lost.

This is a very sad truth. Now, more than ever before in my life I realize that love is truly the greatest gift and the only one that will stand the test of time. Love trumps all the religions of the world, all the beliefs, all the ideas, and all the ideologies.

# Night Vision

The Lord came to me in the middle of the night. It is a night that I will never forget. I even remember what happened before we went to bed that night. I shut off all the lights in the house, including the aquarium light, which was just outside our room.

In the middle of the night I woke up. Light was everywhere, not the kind of light that comes from a bulb, not the kind of light that comes from the sun, it was a light that I had never experienced.

It was everywhere, it permeated everything. If I would have searched for a dark place I would have found none. If we would have had stones for a floor, and if I lifted a stone slightly, I would have seen no shadow. The light was thick.

There was a presence in the room. I knew who it was and didn't think it strange that He was there. I just knew.

I looked over and saw Mary Lynn sleeping. Light was radiating from her as well. And then, without speaking, without using my tongue, I began expressing my wonder and admiration for the beauty that I was beholding. I said, Lord, she is the most beautiful woman I have ever seen, who is she? The answer was, "This is your wife." I was so thankful, all I could say was "Oh, thank you Lord, thank you." Then I rolled over and went back to sleep.

The next day I was troubled. I didn't tell anyone about my vision. I was out in my shop rebuilding a carburetor for one of my hot rods. I was asking myself questions. One of which was: This is my wife. Why didn't I know who she was? Then the Lord spoke to me again. It was unexpected and without lights. I was not aware that He was listening to my thoughts. But He was there and He simply said: "Because you do not know her like I do."

That experience has never left me. It has helped me through the years, to look beyond what is evident in people's lives. God looks into the heart, not the surface, which can portray some pretty rough stuff.

It has helped me to see myself in a different light as well, knowing He

Lonnie J. Good

looks on the inside. He knows who we are! No matter what others think or say of us, it is what He sees that matters.

# Fast Cars

There's been little said about my older sister and the impact she had on my life. One of the most powerful things she introduced me to was muscle cars. She could drive them just as good as any guy I knew. We had some great rides together.

Learning takes on many different facets. While my high school experience left much to be desired, my own desire to know how to do stuff, build stuff, and make stuff was not diminished. My desire to "know" about things most young men take for granted only grew.

With earnings I made while working in the mountains I bought a 1969 Chevelle. While I had owned other hot rods, this car was one of the fastest that I had driven.

It had way too much power for any 19 year old kid. I still remember the feeling of power and the adrenaline rush I got when I pushed the accelerator to the floor and worked my way through the four gears it came equipped with.

1969 Chevelle

Not long after buying the Chevelle, I made a move that looked quite silly to some. I remember when my father-in-law saw what I had done, he laughed out loud and said, "You will never get this car back together again."

I had put it up on blocks in my little shop behind our house and gutted it. When I say I gutted it, I mean, I removed the engine, transmission, drive train, and I didn't stop there. I removed the dash board, and every piece of interior. There was no good reason to do this as there was nothing wrong with the car. The problem was with me, I was sick and tired of being sick and tired of knowing nothing.

I don't recall what I did first but I decided I could build better door panels. The panels from the factory were nothing more than a heavy duty type of card board with vinyl stuck to them with a few shiny strips for trim.

I used light gauge metal which I covered with foam and then black naugahyde with no shiny strips, just black, smooth, and cushy door panels.

I did the same thing for the dash; I used the same metal and formed it to fit in the opening and installed gauges, a speedometer, and stereo. The only difference between the door panels and the dash was the roll and tuck effect that I had sewn into the dash panel.

I took the rear seat out, removing what I saw as unnecessary weight and in its place I mounted some Jensen tri axle speakers that faced directly forward. I bought some really nice carpet and covered the entire floor, from front to back, which went all the way up to the back window.

Chevy 350 Small Block

The real mystery for me was how did that internal combustion engine work?

Rebuilding an engine does not happen over night. It takes a good amount of time and effort to do it right, especially when starting from scratch. There was a lot of time to consider each step. One of the factors that directed me was the price of gas. It was on the rise. As I considered this, I thought that performance and economy should go hand in hand. The deciding factor as to how much of either I wanted to use was directly affected by the pressure on the gas peddle and how often I would use that pressure. It made sense that to build an engine that would squeeze the most from each drop of gas, would also result in the most power as well.

I did get the car back together and drove it for many, many years. It was my commuter, my toy, my hot rod, and a wonderful opportunity to learn.

It would absolutely scream. One of my favorite things to do with it was to drift corners. It had so much power that I didn't need to drop gears, just press down and those rear tires would break lose, then it was a balancing act between the throttle and the steering wheel.

The Jensen tri axles that were being pushed through a great stereo, mixer and amp, would not be trumped by the growling 350. The music and the engine together made a sweet sound that was only heightened by the thrill of squeezing every horse power out of that small block Chevy.

During this time I met John Ray. He was like one of my early guitar mentors, only his expertise lay in mechanics. I truly believe he was more than just a mechanic. He was a borderline genius.

He told me of his younger years. He would be working on something in the shop with his dad. When he came to his dad with a question as to how something worked or how to fix it, he was told, "Go figure it out."

At that point in time his dad was building engines for A.J. Foyt and Parnelli Jones when they were still driving the USAC racing circuit. I knew I was in good hands.

The 69 Chevelle proved to be a great success in so many ways. When I kept my foot out of the throttle I was able to get as much as 30 miles to the gallon. On the other hand, when I wanted to pass someone, I simply pushed the peddle down. Building that car began a long love affair with hot rods. Shortly after building the 69 I found another car that was another great journey into what joy could be had at the end of a wrench and a little hard work.

We took a 1964 Chevelle Malibu Super Sport and made a crazy car. While my 69 was fast, and what I call "long legged," due to the differential that was used, the 64 was quick. It would snap your neck in all four gears.

It had a 4:56 posi track with a stroked 283 c.i., small block. We installed disc brakes on the front. Stock brakes on cars of that vintage were mushy, so that was a much needed improvement. We added a tunnel ram, topped with a set of Holly 600 c.f.m. carbs, which required a little hood modification.

I wish I still had this one, but truth be known it was probably good that I sold it. I don't know that I held enough restraint and wisdom to keep me in one piece at that time.

1964 Chevelle Malibu Super Sport

Adding fuel to my want for fast cars was our involvement at Skagit Speedway Motor Sport Way. I was working each Saturday night as a fire fighter on the track.

Open class sprint cars were the highlight of the raceway. It was a 3/8 clay oval with some pretty steep banked turns. I remember standing in the middle of one of those turns one night. I had jumped out onto the track to check for fire from a wreck before yellow flags were out. Down the back stretch came one of those thundering sprint cars. They top over 100 mph in that spot. I was heading back to my perch on the south turn and realized I couldn't make it. I stood frozen in the middle of turn 3 and got a real close up of what a full blown sprinter looks like in the turn. He had seen me and was off the fuel, but it was still way to close for comfort.

Theo Denny, our family friend, was the main medic on the race track for over 20 years. Before I was on the fire crew I would ride down into the pits with Theo. I would just hang with him. Theo had been a medic in WWII. His position at Skagit Speedway was a great fit for him.

Theo loved his place there, and the drivers were always glad to see him if they were hung up in a bunch of twisted metal. Everyone knew where Theo stood, not just on the front bumper of the ambulance, watching intently for any signs of trouble, but more than that. They knew where he stood in regard to his faith and belief in God. He would pray for them, right there in the dirt or on the gurney. It seemed that when these guys didn't know how things were going to turn out, they didn't mind at all his very open and honest prayers for their broken bones and whatever else they needed.

Theo began teaching me to drive when I was around 13 or 14 years old. There were trips from our home on Township street up to Wickersham, where his mom, Addy, lived. It was a narrow highway which was used heavily by log trucks.

Theo was also my "God" man; he was much focused. He packed his Bible wherever he went. He would never hesitate to pray for anyone who needed it. There were times that I would seek him out to offer up a prayer on my behalf. There was no doubt in my mind that God listened to Theo.

# Wings For Christ

While still attending Burlington Foursquare I met an evangelist who came from Texas. His name was Max Grandfield. After learning of my desire to fly and to be in aviation, he told me about a missionary organization in Waco called Wings For Christ. He encouraged me to go "spy out the land" and to meet the founder, Keith Hull.

I contacted Keith, who was positive, personal and as uplifting as any person could be. He also encouraged me to "come and see." It was hard to contain the excitement I felt as the opportunity to learn to fly and to participate in aviation missions lay at my feet. All I needed to do was stoop down and pick it up.

I rallied and put together the funds for a plane ticket. I flew into Dallas-Fort Worth where I met up with another young man who was also on his way to WFC. Keith said, "The way you will know him is that he will be holding a Bible in the air." I was to do the same. We met, and though a little uncomfortable with that type of "showing," it was fun and there was no doubt that we had found the right person in the Dallas-Fort Worth Airport.

Keith was a small man, somewhat thin due to an illness, but his spirit was larger than life. I was welcomed into his home. I lived with him and his wife, Barbara, for the next couple of weeks. He was an easy man to love. I gained a very deep respect for him during this time.

It became very evident that he was a man of faith, trusting God for everything. He told me stories of his journey and how he had come to be the overseer of this missionary organization.

He loved music and had made an album of some of his most beloved hymns. The extraordinary thing was that he sang all four vocal parts on the album. The name of the album was "Sweet Jesus."

Wings For Christ (WFC) was established in 1961, from that time they were training pilots, at no or little cost. Keith believed that "God would provide."

He practiced his faith and didn't just talk it. He told me of one great step, when he and his partner met with a bank, which owned this old dilapidated airport that is now home base for WFC. He told me that between the two of them, they had 35 cents.

They were looking at a loan cost of somewhere around $700,000 for the acres on which the airport was located.

He believed it could be done with God's help. He gathered a number of veterans together who were all interested in aviation. With their VA loans, they all bought or agreed to buy lots along the airstrip, leaving the strip itself and some area at one end for aircraft parking, office, and housing.

He told me, each step in the process seemed to be done with the last dollar they had at the time. Everything from surveying to short platting and securing the loan, each step was one of faith.

His program was simple. If one was interested in becoming a missionary pilot you would attend his ground school/Bible study that he held at his church. If you completed that 6 month program then one would come out to the ranch for further training and introduction to the aircraft, a Cessna 150, name "Gracie Bird."

There were regular mission trips into the heart of Mexico where supplies, clothes, and even dentists would go to help the much less fortunate. It seemed to me that this was the epitome of real, pure religion. They were actively seeking out the fatherless and widows, then meeting their most fundamental needs.

I was captivated by Keith's love of and for humanity, and his unwavering dedication to mission aviation. I had found where I needed to be.

I returned home knowing that our path had been set. I knew beyond any shadow of doubt that I needed to spend some time helping Keith.

My enthusiasm was quickly doused by the elders in the Foursquare church we had been attending. In short, they said I was not prepared, in any way shape or form, for such an endeavor. My heart went dormant.

The next couple of years were difficult. Our church went through some tough times dealing with members who were leaving "organized" religion and reaching beyond the norms. It was a time of young men beginning to think and express their own understanding of Scriptures.

One of the members that left was my good friend Mark. I was told that I should not contact him. I could not see how banning contact with one considered my brother could be right. I ignored the ban and set out to hear and try to understand what prompted him to take his stand.

We began meeting in our home, looking at Scriptures, singing songs and sharing our lives. But I was restless. I was planning on moving to the east side of the mountains and becoming a river guide, something I had been dabbling in.

We had some friends who were in need of a home so we handed our lease/purchase option over to them as we prepared to move. Just weeks before moving I called Keith; He said, "Lonnie, we've been waiting for you."

Even though I had almost given up on my dream of moving to Texas to help Keith, when I heard his voice, when he said, "Lonnie, we've been waiting for you," it was as if the dams that kept my tears from flowing were broken. My heart knew that I must go.

We were already all but packed. I had previously bought an old school bus, which we had been using on our musical endeavors. We had been doing concerts around the local area.

We loaded what we could fit into the bus, which we also equipped to tow an old one-ton truck. My wife, Mary Lynn, would drive the 65 Impala which was equipped to tow the small horse trailer. It was loaded with horses. I imagine it was quite a sight to many. The old bus would only do 55 and that was downhill with a good tail wind.

It took us two weeks to make the trip to Waco, Texas. We were pretty close to being broke by the time we got there. Our calculations were close; we knew what the fuel cost would be but we couldn't foresee the breakdowns that we experienced.

I had to part with a pair of old Chevy "194" fuelie heads that I had been saving for my next hot rod. I traded them to someone in Arizona for a radiator for the Impala. These were the same fuelie heads Bruce Springsteen mentioned in his song, "Racing In The Street." "I've got a 69 Chevy with 396, fuelie heads and a hurst on the floor."

Once we reached our destination, housing was supplied in the way of an old single-wide trailer. It needed some work, but so did everything there.

It didn't take long to dive into the middle of all the projects around us. There were stables, where local folks kept a few horses. That fit Mary Lynn's profile, so that was her gig.

The grounds needed some care, everything from fencing, plumbing, mowing, cleaning, and organizing. I don't know that I ever felt as content in my entire life. I was part of something. Something that gave me a way to honor my dad and God, all at the same time.

# Facing Fear

Dad and I in May 1964; he died in June.

The stench of aviation fuel permeated the air. I knew the wreckage could ignite at any moment. It was not fire but peace and serenity that engulfed me. I reached through the gaping hole in the side of the fuselage that I had just crawled through and began pulling my friends and fellow missionaries to safety.

Twenty two years earlier, Father's Day 1964, my grandfather burst through our front door, grasped my mother, held her, and sobbed. After a while he came to me with tears running down his face and said, "Son, you are the man of the house now. Your dad is not coming home."

Before the tears came, even before I could mourn, my path had been set. Dad had given his life in the service of others and somehow I knew that it fell to me to carry on in his footsteps.

His Father's Day cake was sitting untouched on the kitchen table. Two days prior, I had chosen it from a rack in the bakery truck that delivered bread to the family farm.

He flew over the farm that day, rocking the wings of the small plane. This was his way of saying, "I see you son." With wonder and admiration I waved and watched till he was out of sight.

He was on his way to join others in a search for a downed plane. This was no different than all the other searches he had been on as a volunteer with the Civil Air Patrol. None of us had any way of knowing the impending circumstances or chain of events that would forever alter our lives.

While searching, they spotted what appeared to be wreckage. Flying too low and without adequate power to climb, the small plane they were flying slammed into the side of the mountain.

I remember being told that the pilot had seen angels appear and kneel at my father's head as he died. Whether this actually happened or if they were merely words to comfort a little boy, I do not know, but I do know that I have told that story a thousand times, and a thousand times there were angels.

The next time I saw him, his body was cold and lifeless. I reached into the casket and touched his hand and saw the scars beneath the wax and make-up that was used to cover his torn flesh.

My father was twenty eight years old when he died. Despite the fear that I too would die at that age, I placed my life in God's hands.

At age twenty eight I was in Waco, Texas with a missionary organization called "Wings For Christ," helping them and receiving the necessary training to pursue my lifelong dream of being a missionary pilot.

Our mission took on many different forms. On this particular trip we were to deliver a pickup truck to a native missionary down in Mexico. We would then return by small plane to the U.S.

The afternoon was hot and muggy at the high altitude airport in the heart of Mexico. Standing on the tarmac of Del Norte airport, we tossed a coin to see who would ride in the cramped rear compartment. Having lost, I crawled through the small door and buckled myself in, giving the seat belt an extra pull, as if to prepare for the unexpected terror that lay ahead.

The prospect of my own death haunted me. Today was my twenty-ninth birthday, the last day of my life that these fears could come to pass.

For the last couple of years I had been praying that God would not allow me to be taken this way. I did not want my two young children to know the loneliness and pain of growing up without a dad, no one to play catch with, no dad to cheer a home run, no one to take them fishing. I wanted to be the dad that I never had.

Our first attempt to take off should have been a warning as the aircraft veered off the runway to the left. We stopped and tried again with the same results. The pilot requested a longer runway. Permission was granted and the tower asked if everything was okay. We replied in the affirmative, and our third attempt to get off the ground was successful. However, the initial feeling of freedom from the earth was short lived.

We were climbing and almost clear of the air field when the airplane began to falter. The pilot had to drop the nose slightly to keep us flying. The airplane again started to fall, and again the pilot was able to correct enough to keep us airborne. Both men in the cockpit were trying desperately to regain control and avoid the crash that would surely kill us all.

Other than the engines roaring and the warning horn sounding, things were quiet. No one was yelling. No one said a word. The airplane stalled and turned hard to the left. We were falling. I looked out the window and saw the ground rushing up to meet us. Quietly I said, "Father, protect us." Had we hit the ground at that angle we would have died.

At the instant the left wing was going to hit the ground, I heard the co-pilot cry out, "Oh my God," and then we collided with an old abandoned cargo plane sitting at the end of the runway. Our trajectory had been altered; now we were doing a flat spin through the air until we hit the ground.

As we were spinning through the air, for me, time stopped. God opened up a veil and allowed me to look into heavenly places. The most detestable, black creatures were standing side by side in a place where they were allowed to come and argue their cases against humanity. I was permitted to see only their backs. I was not required to see how hideous they really were. They were bargaining for our lives. All of this happened in a fraction of a second. God said, "NO!" He denied their appeals to let us die. I knew in my heart, that God's "NO" was the result of my prayers. It was over. I unbuckled my safety belt and crawled out of the wreckage.

"God was here."

After being pulled to safety, the crew was loaded into aid units and taken to hospitals. Alone, I walked through the crash site and took pictures of the wreckage. With only a small scratch and an ear-to-ear smile, I was asking myself, "Why are you smiling so?" It was then that I realized what had just happened. God was there, God was great, and God had delivered me. I do not remember how long I was in a state of euphoria and though it took a few days for the sore muscles to heal, the impact of that moment has never worn off.

Each time I fly, I think of the all-encompassing grace of God. The fear is gone. I love flying, and I love taking children up and watching their faces as we lift off the runway.

2DR / EL NORTE / Lunes 7 de Julio de 1986

## Seguridad Pública

# Entre risas retrata avioneta que pudo causarle la muerte

### Por JOSE LANDEROS

Entre risas, Lonnie Good pidió ayer una cámara para retratar los restos de una avioneta que chocó contra la cabina de un DC-3, después de que el mismo estuvo en peligro de perder la vida en ese accidente con otros cuatro turistas norteamericanos.

Un guardia del Aeropuerto del Norte dijo que los ocupantes de la avioneta Cessna 320 parecían estar tomados, pero esa versión no se confirmó con los partes médicos.

A sólo un minuto de que despegó, la avioneta se tambaleó en el aire y se proyectó contra la cabina de un antiguo DC-3 que décade hace tiempo está abandonado a unos metros de la pista número 20.

La avioneta de seis plazas y con matrícula N574RX quedó destruida a unos metros del DC-3 como a las 16:15 horas.

En pocos minutos se concentraron en el Aeropuerto del Norte ambulancias de la Cruz Verde de San Nicolás y de la Cruz Roja de Monterrey para auxiliar a cuatro de los cinco turistas, quienes ingresaron a la Clínica 6 del Seguro Social.

La comandancia de la Cruz Verde informó que su personal levantó del lugar del accidente a los norteamericanos Gregory Dail Smith, de 26 años, Phil Little y Don Hix, quien piloteaba la avioneta.

El personal de la Cruz Roja, por su parte, auxilió a Don Holland, de 51 años, quien resultó con una herida en la reja derecha y probable

hasta que nos estrellamos", explicó Holland.

Al lugar acudieron los agentes de la Policía Judicial Jesús Sánchez y Leopoldo González al mando del comandante Miguel Delgado, quienes realizan investigaciones para descartar que los norteameri-

canos transportaran droga.

Anselmo Castillo Betancurt, jefe de aeronáutica del Aeropuerto del Norte, informó que la avioneta iba con destino a Nuevo Laredo y que al despegar a las 16:15 horas por la pista número 20, el aparato empezó a tambalearse y luego se estrelló en el

DC-3.

Las causas exactas del acciden-te, expresó, no pueden ser determi-nadas de inmediato, ya que tendrá que realizarse un peritaje en los mo-tores e instrumentos de la avioneta para dictaminar qué fue lo que ocsionó el percance.

Lonnie Good retrató entre risas los restos de la avioneta en la que él viajaba y que se estrelló ayer en la cabina de un antiguo DC-3. Good sólo resultó con lesiones ligeras.

This article, written by Jose Landeros, was published July 7, 1986 in the El Norte daily newspaper located in Monterrey Mexico.

The clipping on page 65 and the one below are one article.

# Choca una avioneta; deja a 4 lesionados

### Por JOSE LANDEROS

Una avioneta con cinco norteamericanos que iban de regreso a su País chocó y se estrelló ayer durante el despegue que pretendía hacer del Aeropuerto del Norte, dejando un saldo de cuatro lesionados.

El accidente ocurrió cuando el piloto de la avioneta Cessna 320 de seis plazas con matrícula N-5748X, David Hix, se estrelló contra un avión DC-3 que está abandonado desde hace varios años a unos metros del final de la pista 20, por la que intentó el despegue.

Ambulancias de la Cruz Verde de San Nicolás y la Cruz Roja de Monterrey trasladaron a los lesionados David Hix, Gregory Dail, Phil Little y Don Holland a la Clínica 6 del Instituto Mexicano del Seguro Social.

Los tres primeros ingresaron a ese nosocomio politraumatizados y en estado de gravedad, mientras que Holland presentaba únicamente una herida en la ceja derecha y la fractura de la nariz.

El quinto pasajero, Loni Good, resultó sólo con escoriaciones leves y aparentemente en buen estado, ya que permaneció en el lugar del accidente sonriendo y tomando fotos.

Los norteamericanos, según dijo Holland, habían pasado el fin de semana visitando lugares turísticos de Nuevo León, en especial la Cola de Caballo y el Obispado.

Indicó que no podía precisar la causa del accidente, ya que sólo empezó a sentir que la avioneta se "tambaleaba" cuando se encontraba a pocos metros de la tierra, después del despegue.

Indicó que después de esos movimientos bruscos sintió que la avioneta chocaba contra algo y se desplomaba.

Antes de que se enterara explicó, la ayuda ya había llegado y él y sus compañeros fueron rescatados de la nave que quedó destrozada, principalmente en su parte frontal.

El avión DC-3 propiedad de una compañía avícola, según versiones de empleados del Aeropuerto del Norte, presentaba el impacto en la cabina y la nariz del aparato quedó a varios metros de distancia.

Anselmo Castillo Betancourt jefe de aeronáutica del Aeropuerto indicó que las causas del accidente podrán ser establecidas hasta que se efectúe el peritaje correspondiente.

The little boy in me still looks up every time a plane flies over, remembering the time the wings waved. . . and gives thanks for life and a heritage that was given to him by both his earthly and heavenly Father.

# Getting Back On

We have all heard that when you get bucked off a horse, the first thing to do is get back on, which I learned firsthand back on the ranch in Marblemount. Keith also knew firsthand what I needed to do. He had survived several plane crashes, once telling me that "They use to call me crash."

It was not easy to get back into a small plane, and harder still to navigate it back to the ground. There were several times when my instructor, Brad Westom, and I would be over the threshold and I would take my hands off the yoke and say, "You take it; I can't do it."

But eventually, I was able to guide "Gracie Bird" back to terra firma, without hesitation or fear. Thank you, Brad, for your patience with me.

Getting back on also applies to so many other aspects of our lives. For me, I don't know that anything was harder to do than try to move beyond divorce. While it appeared to others that I had done just that, there were times I would throw my hands in the air and say, "I can't do it."

Our time in Texas lasted approximately two years. I came back home in the summer months to drive truck for National Foods. I would send the money south to Mary Lynn.

Keith passed away from complications of diabetes. I don't know that I have ever met his equal when it comes to loving people and living a life of faith. One day Keith was talking to me, and he said, "Lonnie, in all the years that I have been doing this, no one has ever been a bigger help to me than you."

The elders had it all wrong; not only was I ready for that mission, it was one of the best times of my life.

Upon returning home, I set out to gain my Airframe and Powerplant License and to finish up with my private pilot license as well. I wanted to immerse myself into a work similar to what Keith had done.

I found a job in an aircraft fabrication shop in Day Creek, a little known shop that was owned and operated by a distant cousin of mine, Jim Hayton. Jim knew of my dad's crash. He was the one who fueled the plane in which he was flying the day they set out to find the downed craft.

I learned to build Cessna wings while under Jim's employment. It was a trade that I would take with me. One which I am still using and hope to pass on to someone else who will use it well.

We had rented a house nearby, and I walked to and from work. I also finished up my pilot's license and was building up a little flight time as I could afford.

Thirteen years of fighting had taken its toll on our marriage. My life came to a screeching halt, which was not a lot different than slamming into the ground at over a hundred miles per hour, or splitting one's own foot with an axe. Things change… instantly. Other people have to step in and do what you cannot.

I was ordered to remove my belongings from our home by the court, who had granted her custody of the children and the home. I was ordered to pay everything I made to her - well except for $230 dollars each month that I could keep.

I lost my job not long after that and then my truck. But on the positive side I had gained skills and a trade no one could take from me. I began building wings out of a garage in Burlington.

Not long after this time, I re-injured my lower back. I was laid up for a couple years. I took advantage of the down time and went back to school.

This time school was something I wanted. I maintained a 4.0 in that AA program which resulted in my FAA license as an Aircraft Technician. Education is always the right choice.

# Too Soon To Fly

I struggled to get my feet back under me. While still floundering, I met the woman with whom I would attempt a second marriage - Regina Crook.

She was a singer in a local band. While visiting the band at a practice we talked. Several months later I called her. She had a lot of needs and I was raised to take care of the woman, first and foremost. So it seemed like a good match. However, it turned south in such a short time that I cannot in good conscience call it a marriage, but more of an attempt at one.

After two short years I found myself embroiled in a battle for which I was not prepared. We spent the next ten years in court. The first year found me in Skagit County Superior Court each Friday on the civil motions calendar.

She had hired an attorney, who I later learned had built his entire career on the backs of some very good men, whom he would bury in litigation. I am most certain that he turned many a good father into a deadbeat dad, all the while holding the position as an "Officer of the Court," which is what any attorney is.

In our two short years we had two children, Kayla and Jesse. I was not going to lose my children again.

After one of the initial hearings, in which her attorney tried to have me jailed, he met me in the hallway of the court and said, "You will never have custody of your children again."

The following week, he was standing on the courthouse steps after beating me up pretty bad in the court room. I was walking away from the building when he shouted, "Hey, nice tail between your legs."

It took me a couple years to get my second wind and to learn how to do litigation. I would not recommend it to anyone unless you absolutely were pinned against the proverbial wall and had no other options. And if what you were fighting for is worth it.

It was during this period that I was given another gift; it came as the result of what looked to be utter failure. I was working for the Boeing Airplane Group but was caught in one of the downturns, at which time

70

I was laid off. This made me eligible for some dislocated aerospace funds, which I used to gain my second AA; this one was in Paralegal. The skills as paralegal came in handy as I had no idea at all of how to manage this war of words that had been waged on me.

I use to joke that I never dated, I married. So it was, two more attempts at having that "normal" life came and went. At one point while in the midst of the battle, the Lord came to me in a dream. He showed me a woman, and said, "I have someone for you." There were not any words wasted, no bells or whistles, just a face and a very comforting message.

I thought I found her a couple of times but that was just me.

# Time Alone

I would be remiss if I did not include at least one chapter that included one of the epiphanies of my life. One of the defining moments came while in a counseling session, wherein I had agreed to meet with my estranged wife.

That particular session began as others. We were together in the same room with the counselor, Patricia Born. I sat and listened while my estranged laid out her list of wants, needs, demands, complaints, etc... It seemed to go on for at least a half an hour. Patricia looked at me and asked, "Lonnie, what do you need?"

The question caught me off guard. It was as if someone had punched me in the face and I didn't see it coming. I was stunned. I stared at Pat, with nothing coming to mind. I had no answer, not even an idea of an answer. It was the moment I realized that I was broken.

The inability to answer the question sent me on a journey. A journey in which I had to travel into the very heart of who I was. I had to find the broken places that were allowing all of the goodness of life to leak out.

The words that my grandfather had spoken to me some thirty years earlier were coming to bear. He told me that it was my job to care for my mom and my sisters. That concept, without any further instruction, laid on the back of a six-year-old boy had taken its toll.

A friend of mine and his wife, Bill and Gayla Childers, gave me a book titled, "Codependency No More" by Melody Betty. The book was a godsend. I began to realize what I had been doing and what I needed to do.

One of the concepts in the book was the importance of boundaries. It didn't take long for me to realize that I did not have any boundaries.

Boundaries keep your neighbors from dumping their garbage into your back yard, as well as keeping you from dumping yours into theirs. Boundaries keep nations from overtaking other countries. When those boundaries are challenged or when they fail, war ensues. There is not much difference in large boarders around nations or the small fences around a home or those invisible barriers that each person needs around their own heart and life.

Building fences, it doesn't happen overnight. Nor does erecting some form of parameters around one's own personal space. Life doesn't stop while we are in the process of building; it continues to go on.

I bought a little house that was nestled next to a small creek, where Kayla, Jesse and I spent our time. I was learning to be alone, to plant my own flowers and to watch them grow.

It was during this time that I began leading worship at a little church in Lyman. The old mission had long since been torn down, which left the small town with only one small church. It was a Baptist church but it was much more about community than any particular denomination.

It was like coming home. It was the same old building that I was baptized in when I was nine years old. The small congregation had recently gone through a church split and was in need of help.

One thing I learned about myself is that I loved coming alongside and helping. It was a good fit. I began leading worship and continued doing that for the next seven years.

We had an incredible team of musicians. The music was most assuredly not the typical Sunday morning humdrum. We had a handful of great vocalists, several guitars, drums, bass, and keys. We did a lot of original music. These were some of the most rewarding times that I ever experienced, musically.

While serving this church I also began a Sunday morning class on codependency. It was much needed and attended well; people began learning about interpersonal relationships. There was a lot of healing that resulted from that class.

# Solid Ground

The first time Teresa and I met was when she came out to my little make-shift studio to do some recording. At the time, I was in one of those attempts that was not going very well. My estranged partner was living in a separate residence and had been for some time. She had begun divorce proceedings, which I was not looking forward to. I was dragging my feet in responding or acknowledging the circumstances that I once again found myself in.

During our first recording session, I asked Teresa, "Are you in love?" - not so much as looking at her but keeping my eyes on the screen. The words to the song I was recording prompted the question, to which she replied, "I thought I was."

From that moment on I had a new hope. Who was this woman who had a smile that was infectious, and who sang like an angel. What were these feelings stirring in my heart that I thought were long dead?

Our initial session was the only one we had as she kept her distance, knowing my situation. It didn't take long for that to finish unraveling.

It's funny. This place in which I lived, Okanogan County, was in fact the same place that I referred to as one of the arm pits of the world. It was this very place that my first wife had moved to in an attempt to distance me from my children. It was now the place where I found the love of my life.

We have now been together for seven years, and though that in itself is not a lot of time, we have gone through a lot together.

Her two daughters, Kelsie and Riley, were still at home and I had full custody and care of Kayla and Jesse. We saw them all off and on to their lives as young adults. We've bought several homes and have had ample opportunity through very stressful times to look at the other and say, "Hey, this is your fault." But there have been no bad words between the two of us.

My bride has never told me to go get "f---d," which is something that I was accustomed to. She only respects and honors me, even when I am not deserving of such. She endured over a year of brutal attacks from "The Good Wives Club" while they tried to have her fired from her position, where she serves as a labor and delivery nurse.

There are countless examples of how we get along but all of that is really meaningless and could change at any given time. There are wonderful attributes to our marriage, but they are but a result of something so much greater, something that I can trust.

It was the same God that spared me in the plane crash, it was the same one that brought me through the wreck, and the same one that took pity on that little boy with no father and brought men to me that could help. It was this God of "Unconditional Love" that said to me, "I have someone for you." My part is to love her.

# Our Little House By The River

Our little place on the banks of the Okanogan River was little more than a shack on some Indian land, when we first started looking at it. I remember the first time I pulled it up in North West Multiple Listing Service, and telling one of my agents that this was a great deal.

When I moved into the Omak area, I became a real estate agent. For the first couple years I worked as a John L. Scott agent before opening my own brokerage.

When the economy began taking its now famous dive, T and I realized that we needed to make some very drastic changes. We realized that we were living well beyond our means.

This little house was the one I sold to one of my clients. It was his plan to flip the house. It was in desperate need of attention. It had been vacant for a number of years and no one was caring for it. The former owner had died and the family lived elsewhere.

Doug, my client, began working on the interior, painting, flooring, and also started cleaning up the debris that surrounded the house.

I would come down from time to time and view the progress as I was going to help him sell it once his work was complete. Though the house was taking shape, the property was a little overwhelming.

The field was overgrown with knapweed, a noxious plant that grows everywhere in this area. The fences were all down and the driveway was nothing more than a line of mud holes. There was a garage, but it was full of garbage and without doors, windows, electricity, etc...

Whatever the negatives, there was an over abundance of something that cannot be bought, traded, or sold. The property absolutely radiated with peace.

It was this peace that caused me to return time and again. It also caused me to bring T down to look at the property. Initially, she was a little apprehensive as the state of disrepair was still readily apparent. But she, unknown to me, was making her own trips across the bridge and down the drive to sit in one of the old dried and wrinkled up recliners that sat on the front porch. She too had sensed this undeniable peace that permeated the property.

One day, while here alone, I was walking the property. I realized that it was an answer to our needs and prayers. I knelt down in the middle of that knapweed and gave thanks for the property and the home.

Shortly thereafter we began negotiations with my clients. We needed to be on the property so we could devote all of our time to it, so we entered into a lease/purchase option and moved in. We began working on the property while at the same time trying to sell the big home on the hill that was sucking the life out of our finances. The time to exercise our purchase option came and still our house was not sold. We had already dumped a ton of money and effort into the river house. Our landlords could have said, "sorry - day late and a dollar short." They could have capitalized on the work that we had done. They could have doubled their money. They chose to extend our contract.

Against all odds, we did get the big house sold and were able to secure financing for the little farm, either of which was no small feat. The large house was in a price category that was no longer moving in our area as it was over $200,000 and we had only been in it for a couple years.

To complicate things even more was the fact that there had been a moratorium on all properties that were considered "high risk" which included any property within the confines of any reservation. We did not know about this prior to making the deal with my clients.

Once we moved in, the work began. There was not a place on the property that did not need some kind of work. Fortunately, for me, Jim Clark had taught me how to work. Most of the work was by hand. At this point I did not own a tractor or implements. I did own several shovels and put them all to work.

Sometime during this new adventure I heard God's whisper. He said, "Let me bless you."

Things that I needed started appearing. Like the old Ford tractor that one of my clients sold to me for a song and dance. And then another one of my clients, whose house I sold, traded to me a bunch of farm equipment in exchange for a commission that he really couldn't afford. Stuff that I needed began appearing and it hasn't stopped.

It took a couple years to get the grounds shaped up. One of the crowning achievements was the stage we erected in the field, made from used materials salvaged from the old buildings that once littered the property.

T and I performing at Goodstock 2013

T and I both agree that we need to use the property for people. And they come, for music, weddings, festivals, and even fresh vegetables.

The first music festival we held was called, "His Harvest Music Fest." The following year we began our annual "Goodstock Music Festival." Our second annual Goodstock Festival doubled in size and we saw our little piece of property filled with people and vendors.

For the previous two years we had been hosting a singer/songwriter showcase at Salmon Creek Coffee Company, located in downtown Okanogan. The audiences grew and the artists continued to appear. There were times it was standing room only for these small one-hour, intimate, musical moments.

At home, once most of the field work was done, I started transforming the old garage into a studio where T and I could record at least some of the endless songs that we continue to write. The studio was becoming a valuable asset in the community as well.

One of the local contractors, Fritz Ridenour, songwriter, who had performed at our weekly showcase, wanted to do some recording, in exchange for some much needed help with the building projects. I had no money, but I did have everything that I needed, even when it came to finding help with aspects of building of which I had little or no knowledge.

Initially, the garage served as my wing shop as well as studio, but then other musicians began appearing and could no longer fit in the small space.

I moved the wing shop into the new addition, which made room for a larger practice room. That room gave way to 50 seats and a stage where artists now perform for those folks that had come to count on the live music sessions.

Some of the artists that have played our venue include Blake Noble, Rodney Branigan, Tim Snider, Bradford Loomis, Beth Whitney, Andrew Vait, Olivia De La Cruz, and Kate Lynne Logan. Every show has been nothing less than incredible. To see and hear artists of this caliber up close and personal is, in my opinion, the best way to experience this wonderful world of Indie music. It just doesn't get any better than this.

This year marked our first Christmas program, which was sold out and enjoyed by everyone that came. This coming year's Goodstock Fest is shaping up to be even better. Word is getting around that "Good Farms" is an awesome venue that pays artists well and music is appreciated in all its wonderful differences.

As I sit here and contemplate this writing effort, I look out the front window where the wind sock, next to the Goodstock sign, reminds me that I am a pilot and the stage reminds me that I am a singer and a song writer and I look over at my bride and am reminded that I am loved.

Goodstock Musical Festival" every third weekend in September.

We enjoyed talking to Nick Elazar at Seattle's Pike Place Market while he created this sketch. He uses grape seed oil and black ink to create portraits and cartoon characters of market goers. It was a fitting conclusion to a wonderful time. We were there to support our friend's CD release "Rust On The Rails" at the Triple Door.

My hope in this effort is that you, the reader, will be blessed and that you will know that God is one of love and not religion. And this meager effort will help you see that the real lasting differences that you make in the lives of others are with the people you actually spend time with, not those you preach at or to.